JUN 2 6 2007

WITHDRAWN

Author:
John Malam studied ancient history and
archaeology at the University of Birmingham,
after which he worked as an archaeologist at the
Ironbridge Gorge Museum, Shropshire. He is now
an author, specializing in non-fiction books for
children. He lives in Cheshire with his wife and
their two children.

Artist:
David Antram was born in Brighton, England,
in 1958. He studied at Eastbourne College of Art
and then worked in advertising for fifteen years
before becoming a full-time artist. He has
illustrated many children's non-fiction books.

Series creator:
David Salariya was born in Dundee,
Scotland. He has illustrated a wide range of books
and has created and designed many new series for
publishers both in the UK and overseas. In 1989,
he established The Salariya Book Company. He
lives in Brighton with his wife, illustrator Shirley
Willis, and their son Jonathan.

Series editor:
Karen Barker Smith

Editor:
Penny Clarke

© The Salariya Book Company Ltd MMIII
All rights reserved. No part of this book may be reproduced,
stored in a retrieval system or transmitted in any form or
by any means, electronic, mechanical, photocopying,
recording or otherwise, without the written permission
of the copyright owner.

Published in Great Britain in 2003 by
Book House, an imprint of
The Salariya Book Company Ltd
25 Marlborough Place, Brighton BN1 1UB

ISBN-10: 0-531-14974-9 (Lib. Bdg.)
ISBN-13: 978-0-531-14974-4 (Lib. Bdg.)
ISBN-10: 0-531-16999-5 (Pbk.)
ISBN-13: 978-0-531-16999-5 (Pbk.)

Published in 2007 in the United States
by Franklin Watts
an Imprint of Scholastic Library Publishing
90 Sherman Turnpike, Danbury, CT 06816

A CIP catalog record for this book is available from
the Library of Congress.

Printed and bound in Belgium.

You Wouldn't Want to Sail in the Spanish Armada!

Never again!

Written by
John Malam

Illustrated by
David Antram

Created and designed by
David Salariya

An Invasion You'd Rather Not Launch

Franklin Watts®
A Division of Scholastic Inc.
NEW YORK • TORONTO • LONDON • AUCKLAND • SYDNEY
MEXICO CITY • NEW DELHI • HONG KONG
DANBURY, CONNECTICUT

WARRENVILLE PUBLIC LIBRARY DISTRICT
28W751 STAFFORD PLACE
WARRENVILLE, IL 60555

Contents

Introduction

Route taken by the Spanish Armada, 1587—1588

Labels on map:

Many ships are wrecked

August 12. Howard abandons pursuit

Armada flees gale

ATLANTIC OCEAN

SCOTLAND

IRELAND

WALES

ENGLAND

Sept-Oct. 65 ships return

July 29. Channel fights

August 8. Battle of Gravelines

FRANCE

July 17. Storms drive Howard back

July 22. Armada sails

Storm damage

Corunna

PORTUGAL

Madrid

SPAIN

Lisbon

May 20, 1588. 130 ships set sail

April 1587. Drake destroys enemy shipping at Cadiz

It is May in the year 1588, and you are about to set off on a daring voyage. You are a sailor in the service of King Philip II of Spain, and your country is about to send "la felicissima armada" (Spanish for "the most fortunate fleet") to invade England, your enemy. The Spanish Armada is a fleet of ships and its mission is to land soldiers on English soil. Spain's brave fighting men will conquer that annoying little country and then King Philip will be the ruler of England as well as Spain. He wants to change England's religion and to return the country to being a Roman Catholic nation. The invasion will be difficult and as you plot your course, you will soon know if you would—or wouldn't—want to be in the Spanish Armada.

Enemies–Spain Against England

Why 16th-Century Spain Doesn't Like England:

RELIGION. In 1533, Henry VIII of England turned his back on the Pope. King Philip of Spain wants to make England turn back to the Roman Catholic Church.

Spain and England have been enemies for years—ever since King Henry VIII broke away from the Catholic Church and invented the Church of England. Catholics were angry. When Henry VIII's daughter, Elizabeth, became queen and head of the Church of England, King Philip II of Spain was furious. Later, when Elizabeth executed Mary Stuart, he decided to teach the English a lesson. He planned to invade England, but the English found out and on April 19, 1587, Sir Francis Drake destroyed the Spanish ships in Cadiz Harbor. He said he'd "singed the king of Spain's beard"—what an insult!

VENGEANCE. In 1587, Elizabeth I ordered the execution of Mary Stuart, Queen of Scots. Mary was a Roman Catholic who supported Spain. King Philip wants to punish England for her death.

Who's Who?

ELIZABETH I became queen of England in 1558.

PHILIP II, king of Spain since 1556.

RIVALRY. Spain and England both want to control trade with the "New World"—the Americas. English privateers attack Spain's ships bringing treasure from the Americas and King Philip wants to stop them.

SIR FRANCIS DRAKE, an English privateer.

April 19, 1587

Handy Hint
Learn to swim. If you end up in the water, you'll have to swim to safety or drown.

Spanish ships destroyed in Cadiz Harbor

Get Ready! The Armada Gathers

King Philip in Madrid

After El Draque's (Sir Francis Drake's) attack on the ships at Cadiz, your king orders the Marquis of Santa Cruz to assemble a fleet of ships. He will teach those English a lesson! This fleet is the king's Great Armada, which will take an invasion force to England. The king wants the Armada to sail as soon as Santa Cruz has the ships and troops ready—but Santa Cruz has a different idea. The king wanted a surprise attack, but Santa Cruz didn't want the ships to sail in the rough winter seas. Portugal is under Spanish control at this time, so Santa Cruz gathers the fleet off the coast of Lisbon and waits for better weather.

Why hasn't my Armada sailed?

Life as a Spanish Sailor

BAD FOOD. There are maggots in everything, and if you don't eat your food, they will.

SOGGY BED. When it rains, water drips through gaps in the ship's timbers. It drips on you while you're asleep.

NOISE, SMELLS, AND DIRT. It's cramped and gloomy below deck, and it's always noisy, smelly, and very dirty.

December 1587

Marquis of Santa Cruz in Lisbon

His Armada can wait till spring!

Handy Hint

Cheer up, life's not that bad! Drink your daily wine ration— it'll make you feel tipsy and you'll soon forget your troubles.

DISEASE. The bad food and drinking water, and the dirty ship are the perfect conditions for diseases to spread. Check your body for spots and lice.

SICK SANTA. In January 1588, the Marquis of Santa Cruz lay dying of typhus.

9

Cast Off! The Armada Sails

anta Cruz died in February 1588. Your new leader is the Duke of Medina Sidonia, a rich landowner. Would you have chosen him? He's got no experience of ships or warfare at sea, and he's told the king he gets seasick! You hope this is not a bad omen. After a long wait, you finally sail for England. Between May 28 and 30, 1588, the Invincible Armada (as you call it) of about 130 ships sails from Lisbon.

Armada Who's Who?

Commander Don Alonso Perez de Guzman, Duke of Medina Sidonia.

SOLDIERS and SAILORS. About 20,000 soldiers are packed onto the ships. They will fight in England. The ships are crewed by 8,000 sailors, including you.

The Fleet

FOUR GALLEYS and FOUR GALLEASSES. Slaves row these large, armed ships when there is no wind in their sails.

ARMED MERCHANTMEN. Forty of these ships carry all the food and equipment—weapons, horses, mules, tents, and other supplies.

SERVICE SHIPS. Thirty-four small, fast ships take messages between ships and from ship to shore. They will also sail ahead as scouts.

PRIESTS AND SURGEONS. About 180 priests sail with you. They plan to convert England back to Roman Catholicism. In the hospital ship are about 85 surgeons and doctors—in case of casualties.

Handy Hint

Pray for victory. On April 25, go to Lisbon Cathedral, when the Archbishop of Lisbon will bless the Armada before it sails.

SLAVES. About 2,000 slaves row the Armada's galleys.

FIREPOWER. Altogether the ships of the Armada have 2,477 guns of various sizes.

TWENTY WAR GALLEONS. These large, heavy ships have two or three decks and three masts. Each one is armed with about 40 guns and carries about 400 men.

11

Storm! The Armada Is Forced to Wait

The Armada sails north to the Spanish port of Corunna, arriving on June 19, 1588. The ships are loaded with supplies. During the night a storm blows in from the Atlantic, scattering the fleet, which cannot sail on until the storm is over. You discover that the Armada is bound for the port of Calais in the Spanish Netherlands (modern France), where 21,000 Spanish troops will board the ships. They are men of the Duke of Parma's army and the Armada will take them across the English Channel to invade England. Unknown to you, the English know the plan and have sent ships to attack the Armada.

DUKE OF PARMA. He is King Philip's governor-general in the Spanish Netherlands.

LORD HOWARD OF EFFINGHAM. He leads the English fleet and must stop the Armada.

SEASICKNESS. It's the first time most of the Spanish soldiers have been to sea.

Saved by the Storm

THE ENGLISH ARE COMING. Queen Elizabeth has sent about 100 ships to seek out and destroy the Armada before it reaches England.

GETTING CLOSE. The English hope to attack you while you're in port at Corunna.

BLOWN HOME. The storm that scattered your ships forces Elizabeth's fleet back to England. The storm has saved you.

Seen by an English Ship!

You think the weather is on your side. Towards the end of July, a strong wind blows the Armada from Corunna close to the English coast (the same wind that blew the English ships away from Spain). Your ships gather off the Isles of Scilly before sailing along the English Channel. But the English are expecting you. On July 29, Thomas Fleming, on a little ship called the *Golden Hinde*, spots the Armada. He sails back to Plymouth, on the south coast of England, with the bad news.

July 29, 1588

The English Reaction

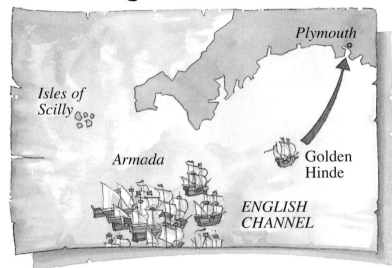

Plymouth

Isles of Scilly

Armada

Golden Hinde

ENGLISH CHANNEL

Handy Hint

Don't let the English take you by surprise. Get your ship's cannons ready for action.

RACE HOME. The *Golden Hinde* takes a day to sail to Plymouth 80 miles away.

BOWLS. Fleming tells Drake the Armada is coming, but he is lawn bowling! He replies, "Time to finish the game and then beat the Spaniards!"

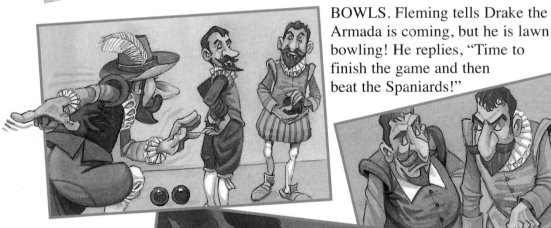

BEACONS. The English light beacons across the country. These fires spread the news that the Armada is on its way to attack England.

ACTION PLAN. The English act fast. Sea captains check their charts, and within hours, their ships leave Plymouth, ready to face the Armada.

BIG GUNS. *Triumph*, an English ship, has 42 guns and is England's biggest ship. On board are 500 sailors, gunners and soldiers.

15

The Chase Along the Channel

The Armada sails in a crescent formation along the English Channel. Heavily armed galleons lead so they can be first to fight the English. As you sail to Calais, to pick up the Duke of Parma's 20,000 soldiers, English ships approach you from behind. El Draque leads one English squadron. The English fire their cannons and some of your ships are damaged. But the worst damage is caused when the *San Salvador* suddenly explodes. A powder barrel ignited and the galleon burns up.

Events in the Channel

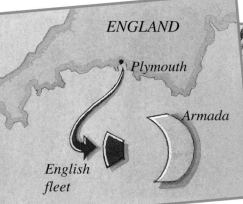

JULY 30. The Armada is sighted off the coast of Cornwall. The fleet is sailing east along the English Channel.

JULY 31. The English fleet, of about 50 ships, leaves Plymouth and chases the Armada along the Channel.

AUGUST 1. Messages of instruction go to each Armada ship. The Duke of Parma is told to move his men to Calais and wait for them to be collected.

16

July 31, 1588

The San Salvador *explodes*

BOOM!

Handy Hint

Prepare for close-range fighting. Climb the rigging with missiles to throw at an English ship.

England here I come!

AUGUST 1. The English seize the wreck of the *San Salvador* and tow it back to England.

AUGUST 2-3. Your ships get close to the enemy. You try to board, but their smaller, faster ships out-maneuver you. They blast you with their cannons.

Boom! Fire the Cannons

Firing Your Cannon

INSERT CHARGE. Collect a charge of gunpowder packed in a canvas cylinder from below deck. Put it down the muzzle of the cannon.

RAM IT IN. Push the charge down to the breech (bottom) of the cannon.

As you approach the Isle of Wight, you are attacked by the English fleet. You must fire back. Your cannon is a culverin—a gun that's 11 feet long and weighs a deck-smashing 4,500 pounds. It can throw a 5-inch, 17-pound iron cannonball a distance of about 400 yards. Unfortunately, the English have more big guns and better gunners than you. You're soon getting low on gunpowder and ammunition. Things are starting to look bad for you and the Armada.

WAD THE CHARGE. Stuff some wadding made from shredded rope down the barrel.

LOAD A SHOT. Roll the cannonball (the shot) down the barrel.

WAD THE SHOT. Pack more wadding into the barrel.

B
O
O
M

ARM THE GUN. Pour some gunpowder into the touch hole (a hole through the barrel to the charge).

TAKE AIM. Move the cannon so it points at an enemy ship.

FIRE! Put a burning match in the touch hole and stand back!

Fireships! The English Try to Burn the Armada

O n August 6, the Armada reaches Calais. Your ships lie ready to pick up the Duke of Parma's army. But the English have a clever plan. Their ships are upwind of yours, which means the wind is blowing from them to you. This means the Armada is open to attack by English fireships loaded with gunpowder and combustible material. The English know you're waiting to collect an army, so that night they send blazing fireships towards you. As these floating bombs approach, everyone panics. Anchor cables are cut and the Armada scatters. In the darkness, many ships collide with each other.

The English fireships

EIGHT SHIPS. One of the eight 220-ton fireships is the *Thomas Drake*—owned by El Draque himself.

Handy Hint

Tie a barrel to your anchor cable. It will float, so you'll know where your anchor is when daybreak comes.

LOADED! The English fireships' cannons are armed, so they'll explode in the fire and do even more damage to your ships.

TAR, PITCH, AND HEMP. Tar, pitch, old hemp ropes, anything that will burn is loaded onto the ships so they'll burn well.

FIRE-STARTER. One man stays on each fireship. As his ship closes in on yours, he sets it on fire, jumps over the side into a rowboat and rows back to the English ships.

21

Shot At! The Battle of Gravelines

As dawn breaks on August 8, you see that the Armada's ships are scattered. Orders come to regroup around Medina Sidonia's flagship, the *San Martin*. As you sail into position, the *San Martin* and three other galleons attack the English fleet off Gravelines, close to Calais. It is a fierce fight. A heavy rain squall blows in during the afternoon and one by one your ships are blown into the North Sea. There is no sign of the Duke of Parma's army and you have no more ammunition. You cannot invade England now.

Battle Tactics

CLOSE RANGE. Your ammunition is low, so only fire close to the English ships—you're more likely to hit them.

GUNS. You're close enough to shoot at the English with your musket—but they'll be shooting at you too.

BOARDERS. If English soldiers try to get onboard your ship, fight them off with your sword.

STOP LEAKS. If your ship springs a leak, patch it with sheets of lead. Be quick or the ship will sink.

Blown Around Britain

It's a relief to be going home, but you can't return the way you came. The wind is against you and the English are behind you. You'll have to take the long route back, which means sailing north up the east coast of England, right around Scotland, and then south down the west coast of Ireland. The weather is on the side of the English and for the first few days they chase you up the North Sea.

Misery Onboard Ship

FOOD SHORTAGES. Food and water have almost run out. You hope they'll last until you reach Spain.

OVERBOARD. The animals that came with you are thrown overboard. They're not needed now, and they'll only drink precious water.

LAST SHOT. You hope the English don't engage you in any more battles— soon there'll be no more ammunition onboard your ship.

August 10-11, 1588

Handy Hint

Keep your spirits up. Sing, dance, tell a joke—anything to stop you feeling as gloomy as your shipmates.

Groan

DISEASE. Men are becoming sick. You hope you don't catch whatever it is they've got.

LEAKY SHIP. Your ship's been hit and water is seeping through the hull. You hope you don't sink.

HOMESICK. Morale is low. Everyone just wants to get home quickly and safely.

25

Wrecked! The Ship Is Lost

It Could Have Been You

The English gave up the chase on August 12 because they knew the Armada's defeated. But you're still in danger. As the remains of the Armada sails around the coasts of Scotland and Ireland, the wind blows the ships towards shore, where many are smashed on the rocks. This happens to your ship off the coast of Ireland.

MASSACRED. Many of your fellow shipmates are washed up on the Irish beaches. Some are caught, stripped, and shot.

HANGED. Those not shot are hanged.

DROWNED. Thousands drown, becoming fish food.

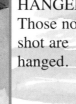

Grab my hand!

Your shipmates who make it ashore are treated roughly by the locals. But you're rescued by another ship—you may yet live to see Spain again!

Handy Hint

Ireland, like Spain, is a Catholic country. If you do find yourself there, ask a priest for food and shelter.

Wreckers at Work

The locals steal anything they can get their hands on, from dead mens' clothes to the timbers of wrecked ships. This is called "wrecking."

27

Home!
Back to Spain

Of the 130 ships that left Lisbon in May, only about 65 limp back to Corunna. You reach there on September 21, but it will be many days before the other ships arrive. After weeks at sea you are war-weary and weak. But at least you've survived to tell your sorry tale. About 11,000 of your countrymen were not so lucky—they died in the ill-fated mission to conquer England.

I'm never going to sea again!

What Happened Next:

KING PHILIP II. He built a new navy for another attack on England.

THE SECOND ARMADA. In 1589, the new fleet sailed for England. But a storm wrecked it and Philip's plans.

QUEEN ELIZABETH I. She was now more famous than ever.

September 21, 1588

Handy Hint

Settle down and enjoy life. One day you'll tell your grandchildren you survived King Philip's "invincible Armada"!

FRANCIS DRAKE. In 1589 he led 150 ships in an attempt to help Portugal get its freedom from Spain. He failed.

LORD HOWARD. In 1591 he attacked a large Spanish treasure fleet, but was beaten. He died on board the Spanish flagship.

PEACE AT LAST. It was not until 1604, during the reign of King James I, that Spain and England made peace.

Index